Quilting
DOT•to•DOT

Patterns for Today's Machine Quilter
Cheryl Barnes

◆ **American Quilter's Society**

P. O. Box 3290 • Paducah, KY 42002-3290
www.AmericanQuilter.com

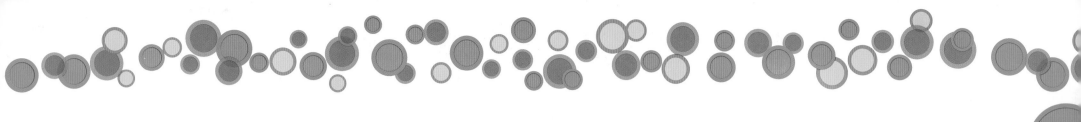

Dedication

To Jim, my husband, for your willingness to follow me into the world of quilting and for your endless support.

To my sons, Jim, Jason, and Ben, for being a constant source of affection, humor, and encouragement.

To my mother, Bea, for showing me the value of hard work and persistence by example.

To my sisters, Marcia and Sharon, and my friends Kathy, Kelly, and Helen for believing in me.

Located in Paducah, Kentucky, the American Quilter's Society (AQS) is dedicated to promoting the accomplishments of today's quilters. Through its publications and events, AQS strives to honor today's quiltmakers and their work and to inspire future creativity and innovation in quiltmaking.

EDITOR: HELEN SQUIRE
TECHNICAL EDITOR: CHERYL BARNES
GRAPHIC DESIGN: AMY CHASE & LYNDA SMITH
COVER DESIGN: MICHAEL BUCKINGHAM

PUBLISHED BY AMERICAN QUILTER'S SOCIETY
IN COOPERATION WITH GOLDEN THREADS.

Library of Congress Cataloging-in-Publication Data
Barnes, Cheryl (Cheryl G.)
  Quilting dot-to-dot patterns for today's machine quilter / by Cheryl Barnes.
    p. cm.
Summary: "Quilting technique for following the quilting path. Patterns for beginner and expert quilters. Designs for sashing, borders with corners, and edge-to-edge pantograph. Tips and hints for machine quilting"--Provided by publisher.
 ISBN 1-57432-902-2
 1. Machine quilting--Patterns. 2. Patchwork--Patterns. I. Title.

TT835.B2666 2006
746.46--dc22
               2006003175

Additional copies of this book may be ordered from the American Quilter's Society, PO Box 3290, Paducah, KY 42002-3290; Toll Free: 800-626-5420, or online at www.AmericanQuilter.com.

Proudly printed and bound in the
United States of America

Contents

Introduction

My love of machine quilting began the first moment I tried a longarm quilting machine. Immediately hooked, I quickly realized that I possessed an eye for analyzing, auditioning, and selecting just the right quilting designs to stitch on my customers' quilt tops. I became fascinated with continuous-line quilting designs and how when stitched they could enhance, and transform, the quilt by adding the perfect finishing touch.

My newfound passion led me to collect and develop a very large library of quilting patterns. Along the way I met and made friends with some very talented ladies who designed patterns for quilting. I was inspired to share these patterns with the rest of the machine-quilting world through my publishing company, Golden Threads. We began to publish quilting pattern packs, stencils, pantographs, wholecloth garment patterns, and books, and developed a line of quilting notions to help all machine quilters. Our original focus was in the longarm world; however, our goals expanded when we realized the rest of the quilting community also needed the patterns and education our talented designers could provide. Our patterns and products can be used by all quilters including hand, domestic machine, home frame systems, shortarm and longarm quilters, and everyone in between.

I am proud to be the spokesperson for Husqvarna Viking's Mega Quilter and Inspira Quilting Frame. This opportunity opened the door for me to reach one of the fastest growing areas in the industry—home quilting systems. Many of the techniques and patterns in this book were especially created as a support for these quilters.

The ongoing Golden Threads Book Series with American Quilter's Society also allows us to fulfill our goal of reaching a greater number of quilters. Each book in the series focuses on the tips, techniques, and quilting patterns of some of today's leading quiltmakers. I am honored to be the technical editor of the series.

Quilting Dot-to-Dot: Patterns for Today's Machine Quilter offers a diverse selection of patterns that I have gathered, enhanced, or created myself. Twin sisters Meredith England and Keryn Emmerson from Australia were the first authors represented by Golden Threads, and they have generously allowed me to include several of their edge-to-edge quilting patterns in this book.

The Dot-to-Dot technique of teaching machine quilting evolved when I noticed a recurring theme of struggles and frustrations encountered by anyone learning to free-motion quilt. Whether quilting on a sewing machine, home quilting frame, shortarm or longarm machine, quilters need to learn to follow the stitching path of their chosen quilt pattern. Machine Quilting Dot-to-Dot takes you through sets of easy to follow "Stepping Stones" that allow you to learn at your own pace and experience success along the way. It is empowering for anyone who has been frustrated or has been afraid to try machine quilting.

My hope is that by combining the Dot-to-Dot machine-quilting technique with a library of quilting patterns and easy to follow Stepping Stones to Success, I have created a resource you will turn to each and every time you are ready to quilt a project.

Remember, It's Not a Quilt Until It's Quilted,

Cheryl Barnes

Chapter 1: Quilting Dot-to-Dot

Machine Quilting Dot-to-Dot

The Quilting Dot-to-Dot technique is an easy to understand method of learning and/or teaching machine quilting that guides quilters through a series of stepping stones towards free-motion quilting confidence.

This quilting technique works on the same principle of the Dot-to-Dot coloring books enjoyed by children and adults alike. In the example below, it is not necessary that you know how to draw a turtle—you just need to get from one dot to the next in the right order to create your masterpiece.

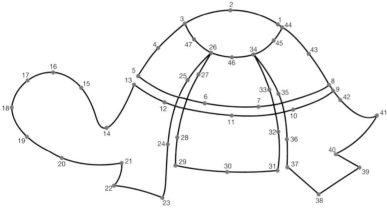

Old-fashioned children's book version of drawing

Machine Quilting Dot-to-Dot works on the same principle. It divides quilting patterns into small sections of stitching, identifies recurring shapes in the pattern, and allows the quilter to focus on stitching just one part of the design at a time.

Notice the stitching paths between the dots are either straight lines or curved lines of varying arcs that flow in different directions. These are the basic shapes that can be practiced using my Stepping Stones to success (chapter 3, page 11), helping you to learn at your own pace and become confident with free-motion quilting.

Eventually your eye will be trained to automatically break quilting patterns into sections and recognize the basic shapes that make up your chosen pattern. You will gain confidence the more you use this technique, and dividing any quilting pattern into stitchable shapes will become second nature.

A new way to quilt shapes by following the dots

Dot-to-Dot

○ Dots divide the stitching path into the basic shapes which can be practiced and stitched as quilting patterns, improving your machine quilting.

○ Dots help identify recurring shapes and design elements when selecting and auditioning coordinating patterns.

○ Dots remain consistent on patterns of all sizes or when the basic shapes flow in different directions along the stitching path.

○ Dots create a focus point for your eyes to move towards, and a target for your needle to reach as you are stitching.

○ Dots can serve as a place to stop, rest, breathe, stretch, change direction, adjust the placement of your hands, and check your progress.

Free-Motion Popularity

The popularity of free-motion quilting has grown to new heights, resulting in techniques, products, and equipment all focused on making quilting the quilt easier for every quilter to accomplish. The unique effects that can be created with planning and auditioning—everything from thread, batting, and quilting designs—have increased the level of recognition of quilting to an admired area of artistic expression, and not just an afterthought to quickly finish the project.

Redefining Free-Motion Quilting

The definition of free-motion quilting has expanded in part because of the growing selection of sewing machines, home quilting frames, shortarm, and longarm machines. All require the quilter to use free-motion quilting techniques. Free-motion quilting is now defined in two ways:

1. Quilting stitched by moving the *fabric* freely in all directions under the needle of any size or type of sewing machine
2. Quilting stitched by freely moving the *machine* over the surface of the fabric by means of any home frame or professional quilting system

Identifying the Building Blocks of Quilting

The three building blocks of machine quilting represent the steps that should be considered as you plan, stitch, and transform your quilt top to a completed quilt. The building blocks remain the same for all free-motion quilters no matter what type of machine, frame, or system you are quilting with.

Building Blocks

○ **Choosing Designs** . . .
   Selecting, sizing, and placing the quilting patterns

○ **Marking Patterns** . . .
   Transferring the quilting pattern to the fabric

○ **Free-Motion Quilting** . . .
   Quilting the stitching path of the chosen pattern

The typical quilter has a "stash" of quilt tops painstakingly pieced, lovingly admired, then gently folded up and stored away. It's time to unfold those quilt tops, select the perfect quilting design, and quilt them into finished quilts. Let *Quilting Dot-to-Dot: Patterns for Today's Machine Quilter* be your guide to releasing your personal style of creative free-motion quilting.

Quilting Dot-to-Dot is for everyone who ever thought, "I'm afraid to try machine quilting . . . I can't stay on the line," or "I'm a new quilter and I can't even stipple!"

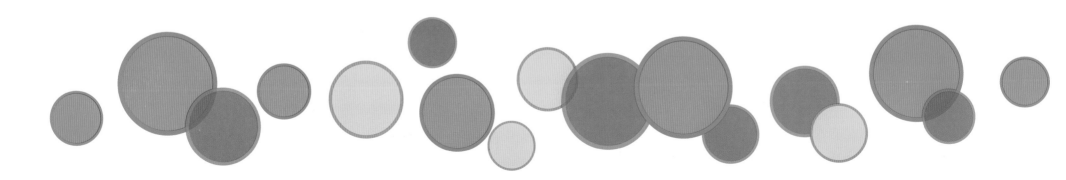

Chapter 2: Building Blocks

Choosing Designs

By the time a quilt top is completed you have invested time choosing the pattern and auditioning a variety of fabrics, making sure the combination of colors, lights, darks, solids, or prints is just right. This planning time insures you will be pleased with your quilt top when it is finished. The next step in the quilting process is to invest time studying your quilt top and exploring your quilting pattern options. Find a convenient place to hang the completed top or spread it out on a flat surface where you can look at it from different angles over a period of several days. Selecting quilting patterns and their placement on the quilt top can become a fun and exciting creative outlet when you see the end results and enjoy the process.

Identify Shapes and Sizes

Begin by identifying the traditional areas to be quilted. Include blocks, borders, sashings, and setting squares/triangles. Trace these areas onto see-through tracing paper or Golden Threads Quilting Paper (see page 110), and pin on the quilt top. Look for unusual shapes and patterns that will fill the outlined area. Create new areas by adding two or more small sections together or dividing a large one into smaller spaces. For quilting pattern ideas, start by collecting clues from the quilt top and the finished quilt.

Tips from the Top
- Is the piecing pattern traditional/contemporary or geometric?
- Does the fabric have a theme or is it seasonal, juvenile, or elegant?
- Will the quilting be the focus or add background texture/movement?
- Is it a scrap quilt, art quilt, heirloom, folk art, or historic quilt?
- Was the top made following the rules for a contest or challenge?

Consider the Finished Quilt
- Is the quilt a gift and, if so, what are the recipient's interests?
- Was the top made for a birthday, anniversary, or other occasion?
- Will it be used as a wallhanging, bed quilt, or baby quilt?
- What thickness and type of batting will be used?
- Is there a deadline for finishing the quilt or time for extra quilting?

Often the same quilt top offers the choice of traditional or irregular-shaped areas. Can you see any more options? Can a large area be divided into smaller sections?

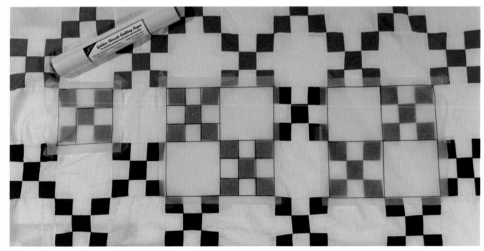

The small and large block choices are easy to visualize. Consider placing designs to highlight the diagonal layout of the pieced blocks.

The two thin borders can be quilted separately or as one wide border. Notice the interesting options for block shapes and/or repeating shapes into one of the borders.

Quilting the small blocks highlights the sashing and cornerstone areas. The larger block patterns create a secondary design when placed side-by-side. This same example also auditions an edge-to-edge quilting design.

- How much machine quilting experience do you have?

Now that you have collected clues from your quilt top, have fun and flip through the following pages marking the patterns you wish to audition. Auditioning a pattern is as simple as copying it on Golden Threads Quilting Paper and pinning it over the area where it will be quilted. It is best to audition a variety of patterns before making your final decision. Below is a list of questions to ask about each of your design choices before you begin quilting:

- Is the pattern sized properly for the area to be quilted?
- Will the pattern(s) evenly distribute the quilting over the quilt top?
- Can one pattern be repeated in different areas or be divided to create smaller patterns adding design consistency?
- Do the designs complement the quilt top, adding visual interest and/or contrast?
- Can secondary patterns be created by placing repeats of the same block or border patterns next to each other?

The patterns in this book have been marked with colored icons that can help you select patterns that coordinate the theme, category, or style of your quilt top. Most patterns fall into more than one category, which expands your options when choosing quilting designs. Have fun, experiment, and get creative!

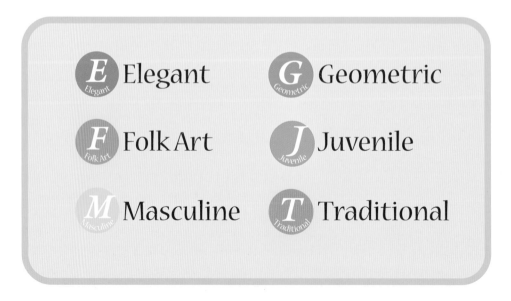

E Elegant *G* Geometric

F Folk Art *J* Juvenile

M Masculine *T* Traditional

Resizing Patterns

After selecting the quilting patterns for your project you may need to resize them to fill the designated areas on your quilt top. The quilting patterns in this book may be resized on a copy machine or scanner (refer to the copyright statement on page 2). To verify that the pattern will fit properly or to accurately resize patterns you will need to take two measurements:

1. Measure the block(s) and border(s), seam line to seam line. For the outside borders, deduct at least ½" for the binding area so the quilting will end before binding begins. Create an inner margin between all quilting and seam lines of ¼" to ½" on all sides.

Example: Block measures 8" square seam line to seam line. To have a ½" margin on all sides your quilting pattern needs to be 7" square.

Example: Your border measures 5" from *seam line to outer edge of fabric*. Your binding will cover ½" and you want a ½" margin each between the stitching and the seams, for a combined total of 1½". The border pattern will need to be 3½".

2. Measure the quilting pattern at its widest points. Borders should be measured from the highest point on the top of the border to the lowest point on the bottom. These points can be in two different areas of the pattern.

The percentage of increase or decrease is needed to change the size of your pattern on a copy machine or scanner. This can be done with a calculator.

Example: The original pattern measures 5" square and needs to be 7" square. The calculation will be $7 \div 5 = 1.4$; $1.4 \times 100 = 140$. The percentage of increase is 140%.

Or use the *Quilter's Assistant Proportional Scale*. The QAPRO has an outer wheel, inner wheel, and a window. The numbers on the wheel are in inches. Using the same example, locate the 5" mark on the inner wheel and turn the wheel until it lines up to the 7" mark on the outer wheel. Look in the window. The arrow will be pointing at 140, the percent of increase. No math!

Always verify that the resized pattern is correct and will fit in the designated area.

Borders create an additional challenge for proper fitting and resizing. After the width of the border is determined, the length of the border and the corners need to be planned and created. Here are several options to make this quick and easy:

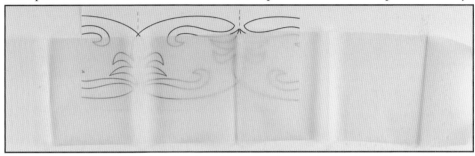

Measure and cut a piece of Golden Threads quilting paper the exact length of your border. Fold in half several times until you have a size that is close to one full repeat of the properly sized pattern. See page 79.

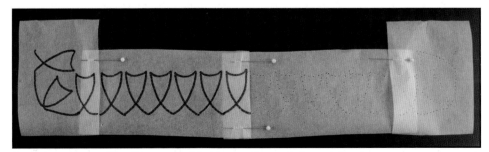

Trace one repeat on the top layer of folded paper. Adjust section to fit fold line to fold line. Refold and needle punch through the folded stack on a sewing machine using a large unthreaded needle.

Trace the corner on GT quilting paper. Machine needle punch through four layers to create corner patterns. Pin in place. Needle punch a stack of individual border sections. Repeat steps for borders to fill area between corners.

Marking Patterns

Quilters everywhere have been looking for a safe and efficient method of transferring a pattern without marking their fabric: The *No Marking Method* uses Golden Threads Quilting Paper, a lightweight, transparent vellum to create needle punched paper stencils that can be stitched or pounced through.

Trace

Trace a pattern onto a piece of GT paper using a pre-tested fabric safe marker or pencil. Draw arrows along the stitching path when the pattern crosses over and changes direction.

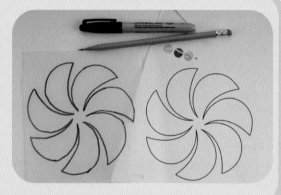

Stitch

Layer up to 15 pieces of paper with the traced copy on top and pin the corners to secure. Using your machine, needle punch through the stack with a large unthreaded needle. Save the traced copy for future use. Consult your sewing machine instructions for stitching without thread. If your machine has a bobbin sensor, try inserting an empty bobbin in place; if the sensor is in the thread path, place a length of thread in the take-up area.

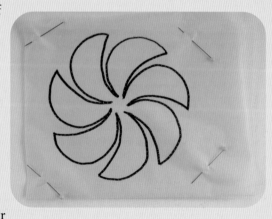

Quilt

Notice that one side of each needle-punched stencil is smooth and the other is bumpy. Turn the bumpy side up and pin or use a temporary spray adhesive to position the tearaway stencils onto the quilt top. Spray the paper—NOT the fabric, avoiding the stitching line.

After basting or before loading the quilt top on the frame, paper stencils can be used when quilting on any sewing machine or quilting system. They can be stitched or marked through with a pounce. This is determined by the color and the print of the fabric being marked.

Tear

For easy removal after quilting, grab hold of the project close to the quilted area and tug on the bias. The paper will pull away from the stitches. Intricate patterns often isolate small sections of paper. Use a toothbrush to loosen and a sticky lint roller to remove any small slivers of paper.

Pounce

Position your paper stencil on your project with the bumpy side up. Using a quilt pounce box with the new Ultimate Pounce® Powder* (not shown), rub the box over the bumps. The chalk will transfer to your fabric marking your stitching path for hand or machine stitching. This new chalk will not rub off when stitching or handling your project. Follow the manufacturer's instructions to simply steam it away with an iron or remove it with the heat of a blow dryer.

* See page 110.

Chapter 3: Stepping Stones

Steps to Free-Motion Success

Learning to free-motion quilt can be intimidating and equally frustrating if you have ever taken a class and have been sent home with the instructions to "just practice." Your next thought was probably "practice what?"

Dot-to-Dot outlines a series of practice exercises—Stepping Stones—that build one skill upon the next, helping you to "baby step" your way to confident free-motion quilting. Think of your progress as the equivalent of teaching a baby to walk.

Babies take their first steps, stumble, trip, and very often fall right on their little bottoms over and over again. The next time they take several steps and fall again. We lovingly applaud and encourage them to get up and keep trying. We are kind and patient, realizing that not every baby learns this new skill at the same age, and some need a little more hand holding than others.

As "grown-ups" we can be our own worst critic, especially if our progress does not match our expectations. Free-motion quilting is a new skill requiring time to practice and progress one step at a time. Just like a baby who falls many times along the way, you too will make mistakes and stitch sections that you are not pleased with. Begin at the first step and move through the Stepping Stones at your own pace. Encourage yourself to keep trying and remember that "falling" is all part of the learning process.

The Stepping Stones Practice Sets of simple designs, pages 12 and 13, are divided into eight basic shapes in three different sizes for your practice. Finger trace several different shapes in the various sizes, and select the shape and size that seem the most natural to you. To grow in quilting confidence, follow these Stepping Stones:

- Finger trace over the shapes.
- Pencil trace the shapes on paper.
- Needle punch the shapes with your machine on paper or on fabric.
- Quilt on a practice mini-quilt sandwich.

How quickly you move through the Stepping Stones is up to you. Skip over any one of the steps if it seems elementary for your current experience level. Do what feels right for you. However do not limit yourself from accomplishing all the skills in each Stepping Stone along the way. Everyone is different—stitching at a different speed and learning at an individual pace—and everyone has a different shape or size of shape that is easier for them. Begin where you are most comfortable!

The Practice Sets on the following pages can be used as shown or enlarged 300% for a full-size practice set. These can also be stitched as your first quilting patterns. Refer to Using the Practice Sets on page 14 for more suggestions.

Edge to Edge quilting-design or border design.

Stepping Stones Practice Sets

Rolling Waves

Zig Zag

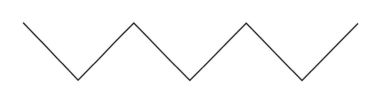

Scallops

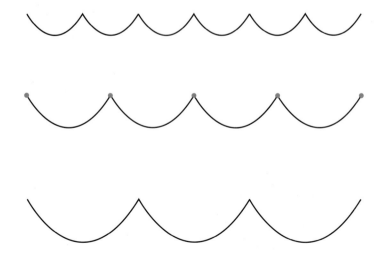

Circles

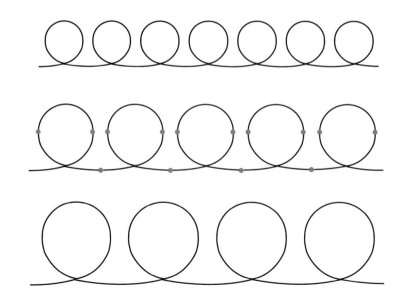

Stepping Stones Practice Sets

Loops

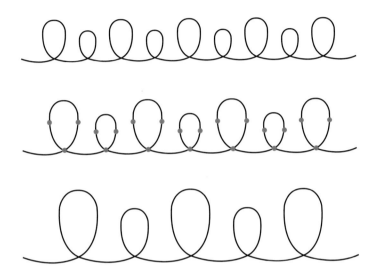

Feathers

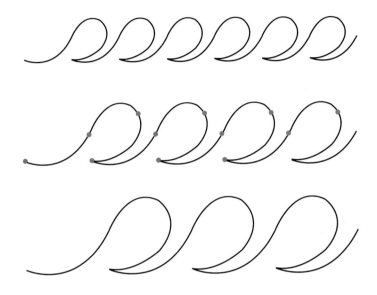

Petal Points

Curls

Using the Practice Sets

Finger Trace

Select a Practice Set from the previous pages and finger trace over and over until you have memorized the pattern. Do this for all three sizes as the flow will feel slightly different as the size changes. Enlarge 300% for full-sized sets.

Pencil Trace

Using paper and pencil, trace your chosen practice shape in all three sizes moving from dot-to-dot along the design path. Trace all three sizes several times until you have multiple sheets of traced patterns. Using a colored marker, place dots where they appear along the design shape in the book. You are continuing your practice and creating patterns for the next step.

Needle Punch

Install a large needle (no thread) in your sewing/quilting machine. Drop the feed dogs. Use the pencil traced Practice Set and stitch following the path of the design. Notice the shapes of each section as you focus on moving from dot-to-dot. Repeat until it feels natural to stitch the design shape in all three sizes.

Add Fabric

Create a mini-quilt at least 18" square using fabric and batting. Trace and needle punch a fresh paper stencil, using the same design shape. Include the dots to assist you in following the stitching path. Pin or use a temporary basting spray to hold the paper in place. Again, stitch without thread following the path of the design shape. Become confident with moving the fabric smoothly, discovering the stitch speed that is best for you.

Practice Quilting

Thread your machine and stitch on the mini quilt. Follow the pattern needle punched on the paper, or traced/pounced on the fabric. Repeat until you are confident following the design shape you have been practicing. This Stepping Stone will help you coordinate the speed you are moving your fabric with how fast you are stitching. Finding and remembering the right combination is key.

Practice Makes Perfect

Repeat the Stepping Stones to learn all the design shapes in the practice section. Each set will help you master a new shape, expanding your quilting pattern options. Look through the patterns in the book, noting which ones incorporate the shapes you have learned. You should have great success and great pride in beginning to quilt them on any project.

The Road to Success

The process of walking through each Stepping Stone may seem time consuming, but remember the goal is to master free-motion quilting by building one skill at a time and celebrating your progress. All the practice design shapes can be used as simple quilting patterns, providing you with a simple selection to begin free-motion quilting on your projects.

Save all the practice mini quilts as a journal of your baby steps, to celebrate your developing quilting skills, and to encourage other new quilters. Proceed at your own pace. Remember this is a lifelong skill—like walking, you need to learn one baby step at a time.

Quilting Warm-ups

Always take a few minutes to warm up before beginning to quilt on your project, especially if it has been awhile since your last quilting session. Create a mini quilt sandwich using the actual fabric, batting, and thread from your project. Use the Stepping Stones that you found to be the most helpful. This will keep your quilting consistent throughout the project. Remember to take breaks to rest and stretch every so often.

Exploring Pattern Choices

When you feel confident with the shapes and patterns in the practice sets, you are ready to move on to explore the quilting patterns. Armed with your new knowledge you should feel empowered to try stitching some new exciting pattern choices.

❍ The practice sets can be stitched as quilting patterns in thin borders or sashings on actual projects.

❍ Your eye should be trained to see these shapes repeated in quilting patterns of varying styles and difficulties.

❍ As the patterns become more complex, several shapes will be combined to create new patterns. Therefore it is best to learn all the shapes.

❍ Quilting with pantographs or edge-to-edge patterns is easier to stitch when you select patterns with familar shapes.

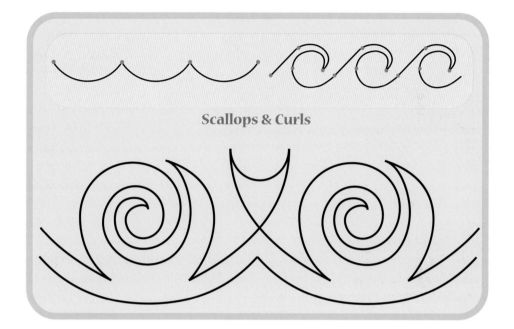

Scallops & Curls

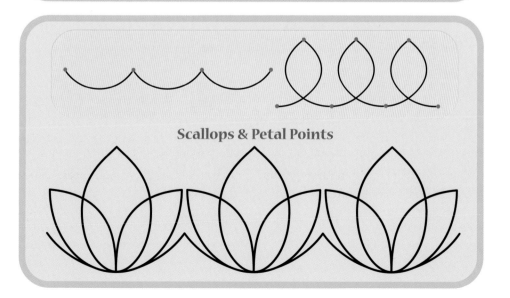

Scallops & Petal Points

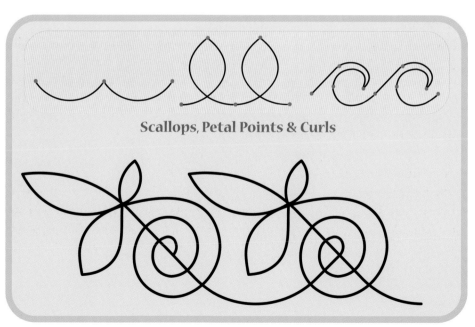

Scallops, Petal Points & Curls

Chapter 4: Machine Quilting Allover Designs

Pantographs/Edge-to-Edge Quilting

By definition, pantographs are 10–12 foot long roll patterns that are followed with a laser while stitching on a quilting frame. Quilting pantograph patterns will cover the quilt edge-to-edge with even lines of stitching. Edge-to-edge quilting does not describe the pattern, but is the description of the type of stitching that results from using a pantograph pattern. However, pantographs are sometimes called edge-to-edge patterns.

Edge-to-edge quilting can be done on a quilting frame or on a domestic sewing machine creating an effect that does exactly what its name suggests—quilting that flows from one edge of the quilt to the other in one continuous line. This is a great way to add texture and movement to a quilt top that does not require intricate quilting motifs or is made from dark and vividly printed fabric where the quilting will not show or be the main focus of the quilt. The stitching can flow from left to right or top to bottom of the quilt. Quilting from the top to the bottom of your quilt requires fewer rows of quilting and less bulk to roll and/or feed through your machine.

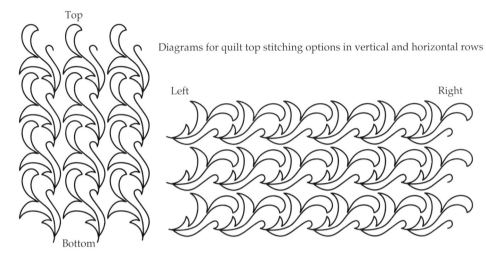

Diagrams for quilt top stitching options in vertical and horizontal rows

Adjusting the Number of Repeats

To avoid quilting a partial row at the bottom of the quilt (for example, 12½ rows) consider the following options:

1. Adjust the spacing between the rows.

2. Change the width of the quilting pattern using the Quilter's Assistant Proportional Scale. (See page 110 for ordering information.)

3. Select a different pattern if the first two options fail.

Making Pantographs

It is important for you to use the alignment lines and dots on the printed patterns to accurately copy, tape, or trace the pattern as you create your pantograph or paper stencil.

You always have various placement options when working with panto patterns. The rows can be mirrored, offset, straight, or reversed by changing the positioning of the pantograph itself. Nesting designs are tucked into the previously quilted row.

Refer to Chapter 2: Building Blocks, page 9, for information for planning edge-to-edge needle-punched patterns, and page 10 for options on transferring the quilting design.

Resizing edge-to-edge patterns

❍ Measure the length of the quilt top.
❍ Measure the width of the quilting pattern and the width of the space between the rows. Add together.
❍ Divide that measurement into the length of the quilt to determine the number of rows to be stitched to cover the top with quilting.

Example:
The quilt top is 48" long, the pattern width is 3½" with a ½" space between the rows. The total is four inches. (48" divided by 4" = 12.) There will be twelve rows of quilting from top to bottom of the quilt.

Quilting on a Quilting Frame
Position the Panto

Unroll the panto on the pattern shelf. Using the needle down/up option, drop the needle exactly where you want the first quilting stitch to begin. Turn the laser on and slide the panto until the light shines on the highest point of the pattern. Place a piece of painters tape to keep the panto from moving. Needle up and move the laser across the top edge of the quilt. Stop and needle down to hold the machine in place. Recheck the position of the laser light on the design. Adjust panto if needed and secure with tape. When quilting a pantograph your eyes are focused on the pattern, not the quilt top. To avoid stitching off the side of the quilt, place tape on both ends of the panto indicating where to stop stitching.

Start to Quilt

Move the machine and drop the needle at your chosen start point. Take several small stitches in place to lock the stitches along the edges where the binding will be attached. Begin quilting by guiding the laser along the pattern until you complete one row and secure the stitches at the end of the row. If the pattern has a second pre-printed row and there is enough space for the needle to reach the highest and lowest points of the pattern, stitch the next row without any pattern adjustments. Use the laser to check these points. Stitch the second row and/or advance your quilt.

Advance the Quilt

Advancing the quilt will roll the quilted area onto the take-up roller, exposing the next area to be quilted.

To determine where the next row of stitching should begin, position the laser light so it is shining on the alignment dot positioned directly under the row just stitched, and needle down to hold the machine in place. Unhook the side clamps and loosen the pole knobs. Gently roll the quilted area onto the take-up roller. Notice the machine will glide as you roll the quilt top. Stop rolling when the laser light is shining on the alignment dot above the row just quilted. Hold the take-up roller in place and tighten the pole knobs. Use the laser to verify the correct stitching

Cheryl is using an Inspira Quilting Frame and the Husqvarna Viking MegaQuilter machine. (Photo used by permission.)

path. If your panto does not have alignment dots, add your own or use the highest/lowest point of your pattern adding a margin of ½" so the rows do not over-lap. See the pattern on page 86.

Free-Motion Quilting Edge-to-Edge Designs

Stitching edge-to-edge designs on a domestic machine requires a stitch line or pounce marks through a paper stencil. There are several options available for you to choose from. Refer to the process and photos on pages 9 and 10 for creating your patterns with Golden Threads Paper.

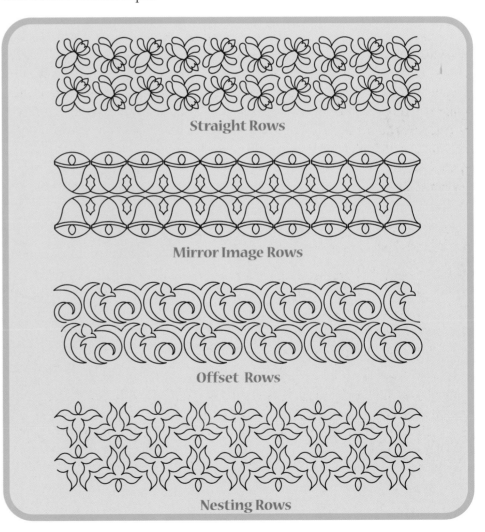

Straight Rows

Mirror Image Rows

Offset Rows

Nesting Rows

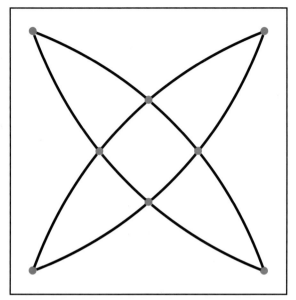

2½"

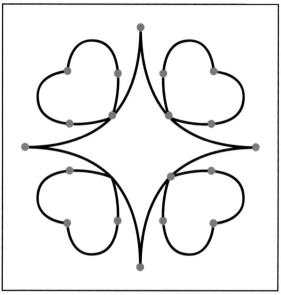

2½"

2½"

2½" — *Design element pattern, page 33*

2½" — *Design element pattern, page 67*

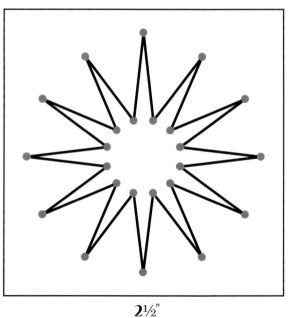

2½"

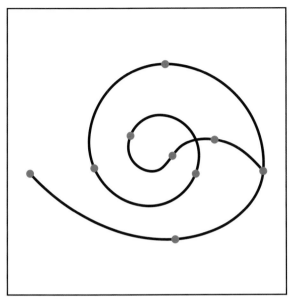

2" — *Design element pattern, page 62*

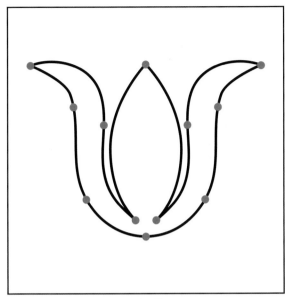

2½"

2½" — *Design element pattern, page 52*

2" — *Design element pattern, page 23*

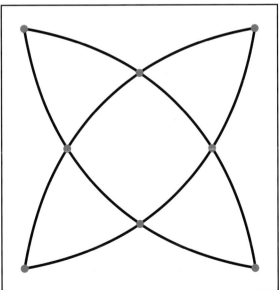

2½"

2½" — *Design element pattern, page 82*

2"

F J T
Folk Art Juvenile Traditional

2"

F T
Folk Art Traditional

4½"

2"

3"

F Folk Art

M Masculine

T Traditional

3½"

E Elegant

1"

E
Elegant

J
Juvenile

2½"

E
Elegant

J
Juvenile

2¾"

G
Geometric

T
Traditional

2¼"

G *Geometric*

F *Folk Art*

M *Masculine*

T *Traditional*

4" – 2¼"

G *Geometric*   M *Masculine*

F *Folk Art*   T *Traditional*

3"

G *Geometric*

M *Masculine*

T *Traditional*

3"

G *Geometric*

F *Folk Art*

M *Masculine*

5"

5"

7¾"

3½"

E *Elegant*

F *Folk Art*

T *Traditional*

7"

E
Elegant

T
Traditional

5"

G Geometric

M Masculine

T Traditional

5"

G Geometric

F Folk Art

M Masculine

1½"

E *Elegant*

G *Geometric*

F *Folk Art*

M *Masculine*

6"

E *Elegant*

G *Geometric*

F *Folk Art*

M *Masculine*

5"

5"

Stitching Sequence

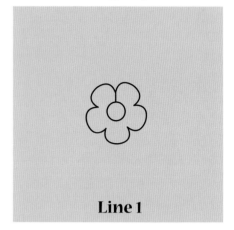

Line 1

Line 2

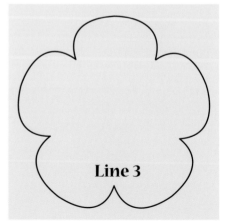

Line 3

6"

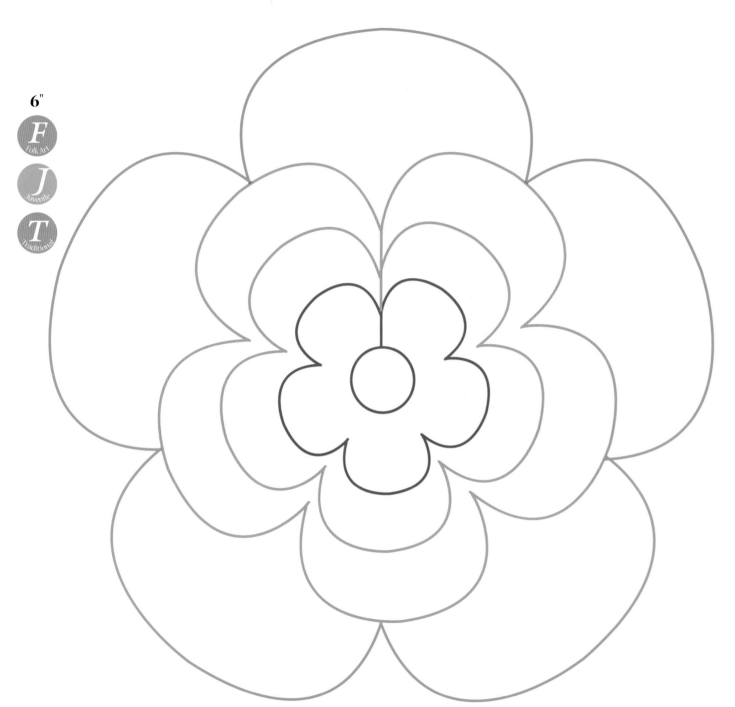

Stitching Sequence

Line 1

Line 2

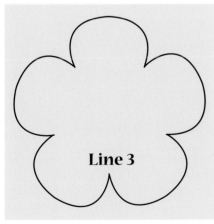

Line 3

6"

E *Elegant*

F *Folk Art*

J *Juvenile*

Stitching Sequence

6"

F *Folk Art*

J *Juvenile*

T *Traditional*

Line 1

Line 2

Line 3

Line 4

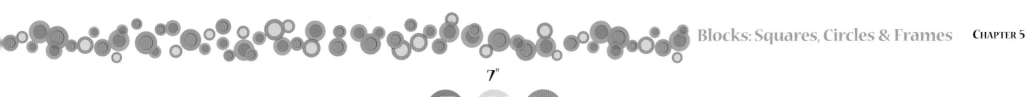

7"

Secondary Design

2½"

F *Folk Art*

M *Masculine*

J *Juvenile*

3¾"

J *Juvenile*

M *Masculine*

5½"

F Folk Art

J Juvenile

M Masculine

2½"

F Folk Art

J Juvenile

M Masculine

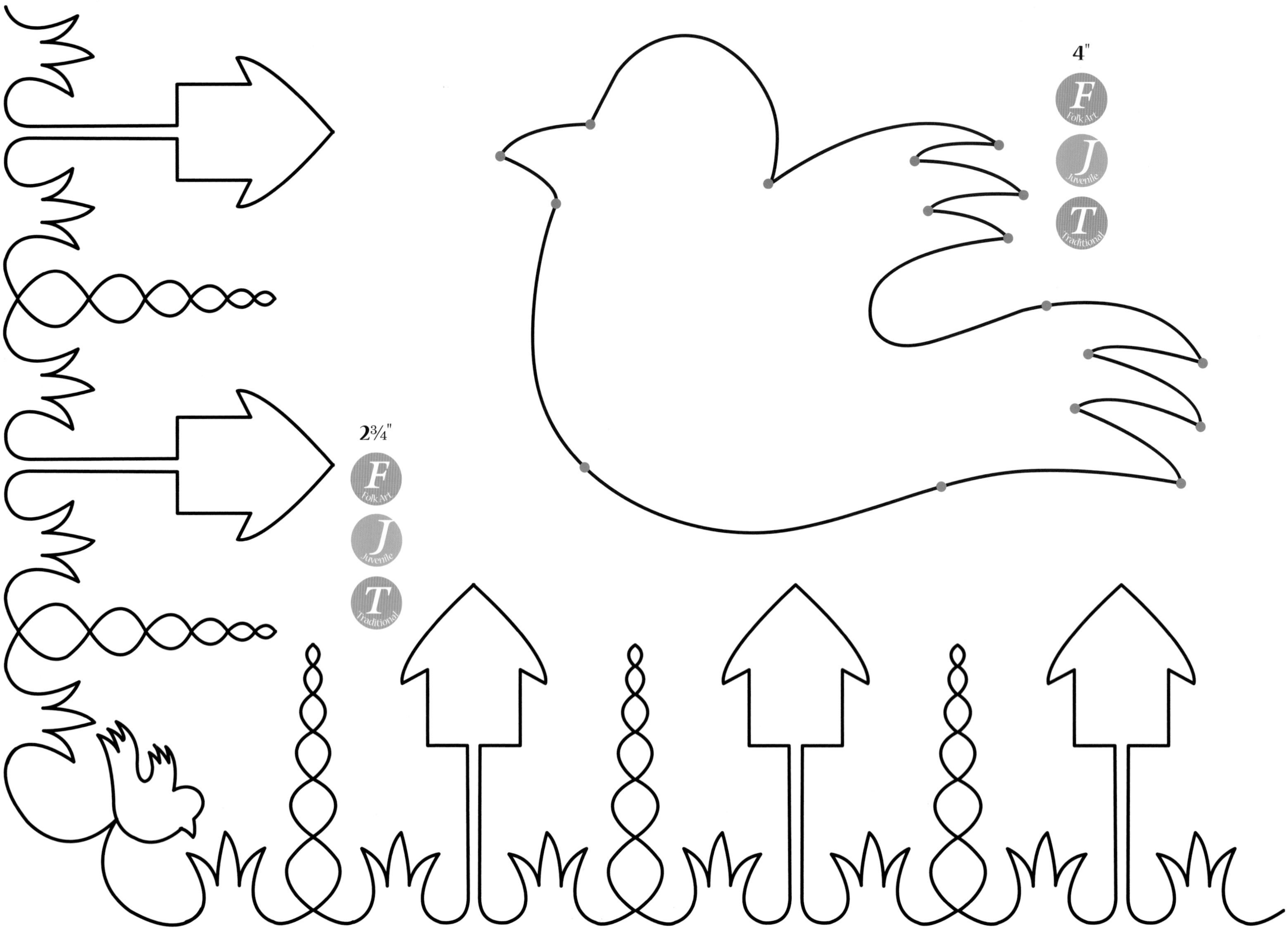

4"

F Folk Art

J Juvenile

T Traditional

2¾"

F Folk Art

J Juvenile

T Traditional

2½"

E Elegant
F Folk Art
J Juvenile
T Traditional

7"

E Elegant
J Juvenile

2½"

F Folk Art

J Juvenile

T Traditional

5"

E Elegant

F Folk Art

J Juvenile

T Traditional

5½"

G
Geometric

F
Folk Art

J
Juvenile

2"

F
Folk Art

J
Juvenile

M
Masculine

T
Traditional

2"

3"

6½"

2¾"

E
Elegant

M
Masculine

T
Traditional

4"

F
Folk Art

J
Juvenile

2¾"

F Folk Art

M Masculine

T Traditional

3½"

G Geometric

F Folk Art

J Juvenile

T Traditional

2½"

G Geometric

F Folk Art

J Juvenile

T Traditional

2"

E
Elegant

F
Folk Art

J
Juvenile

T
Traditional

4"

E
Elegant

F
Folk Art

J
Juvenile

T
Traditional

7" **E** **G** **T**

3" **E** **G** **T**

6"

2"

3½"

4"

F
Folk Art

T
Traditional

2"

F
Folk Art

T
Traditional

7"

G *Geometric*

F *Folk Art*

M *Masculine*

T *Traditional*

Background Fillers

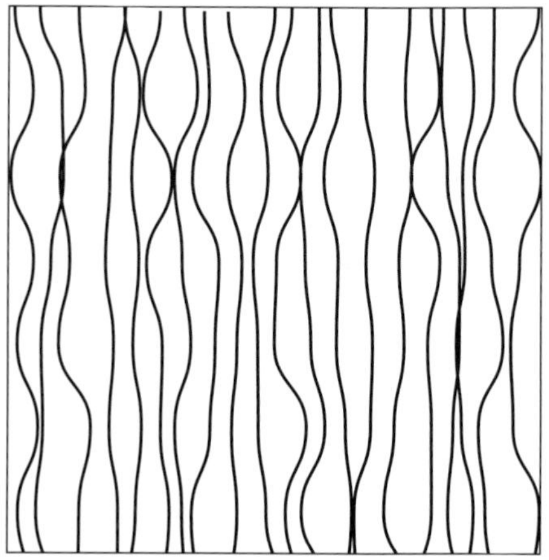

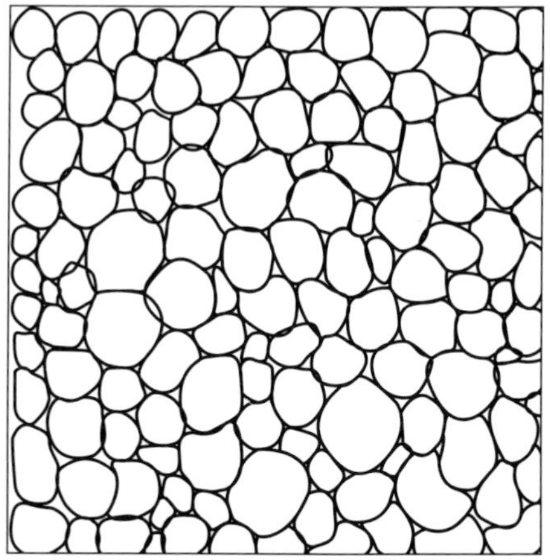

7"

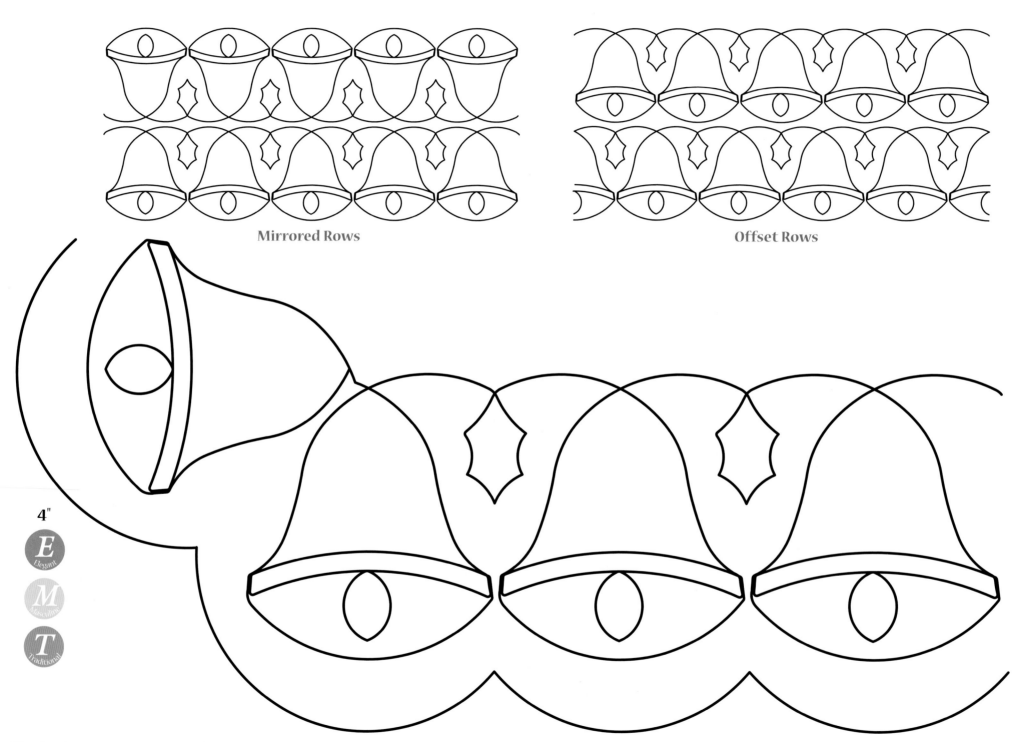

Mirrored Rows

Offset Rows

4"

3"

F *Folk Art*

J *Juvenile*

T *Traditional*

4½"

5"

G Geometric

F Folk Art

M Masculine

2" G Geometric F Folk Art M Masculine

2½" **G** **F** **M**

3" **G** **F** **M**

5"

Outward Design Element

Inward Design Element

5"

Reversed and Nesting Rows

Reversed Rows

5"

5"

Outward Design Element

Inward Design Element

5"

3"

2"

5"

Outward Design Element

Inward Design Element

5"

2"

E G F

3"

E G F

2"

3"

5"

5"

2½"

E G F M T
Elegant Geometric Folk Art Masculine Traditional

2"

E
Elegant

G
Geometric

F
Folk Art

M
Masculine

T
Traditional

3"

7"

Secondary Design

7"

E *Elegant*

F *Folk Art*

T *Traditional*

3"

Inward Design Element

Outward Design Element

2" **G** **F** **M** **T**

Mirrored Rows

4"

Straight Rows

5"

E *Elegant*

M *Masculine*

T *Traditional*

6"

E *Elegant*

M *Masculine*

T *Traditional*

7½"

E Elegant

F Folk Art

T Traditional

4"

E Elegant

F Folk Art

T Traditional

6"

Inward Design Element

Outward Design Element

6"

7"

Reversed Rows

3½"

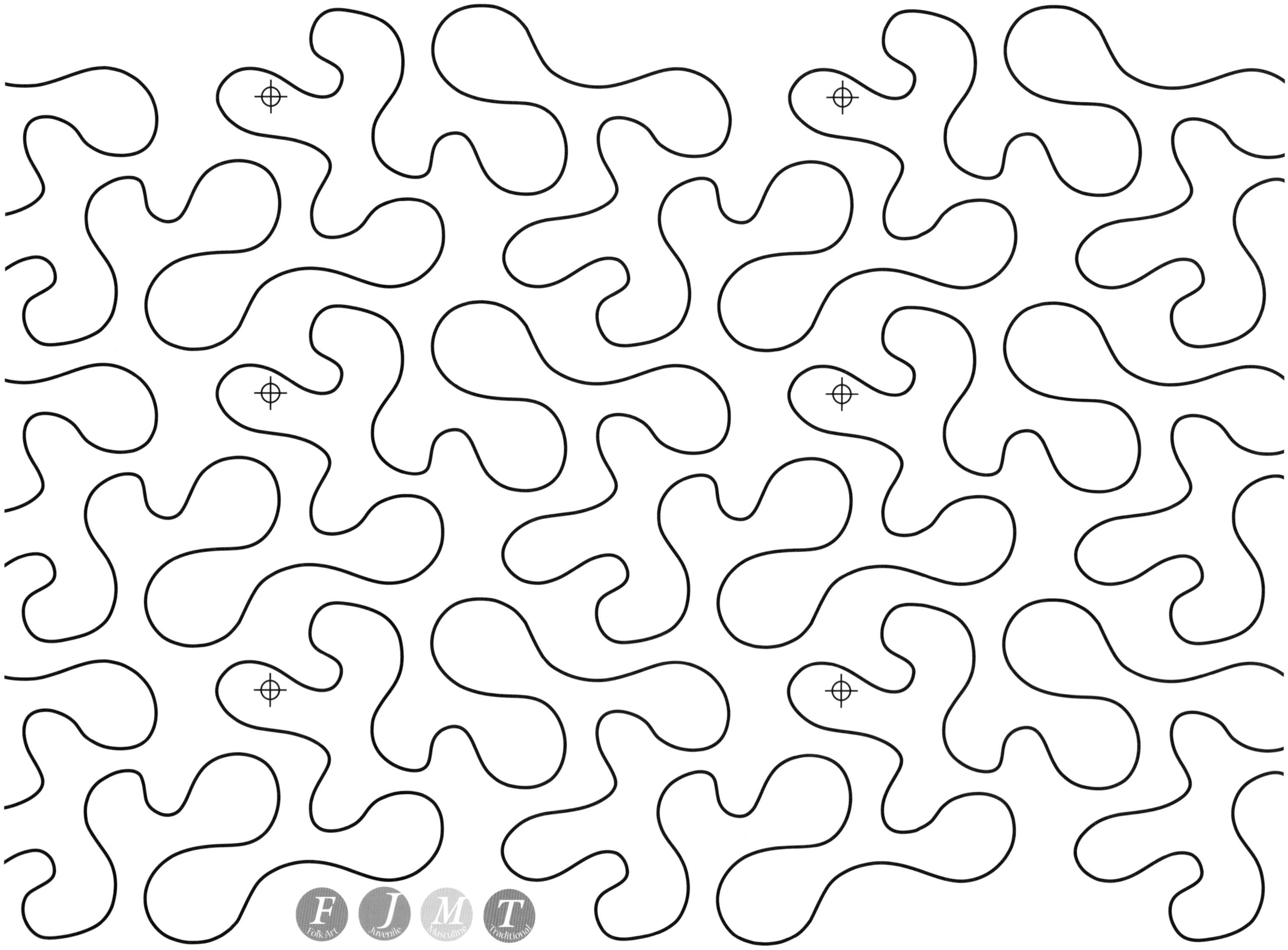
F
Folk Art
J
Juvenile
M
Masculine
T
Traditional

7"

4"

G Geometric

J Juvenile

T Traditional

3" **G** Geometric **J** Juvenile **T** Traditional

4" **E** **F** **M**

3" **E** **F** **M**

4"

E Elegant

F Folk Art

T Traditional

3"

E Elegant

F Folk Art

T Traditional

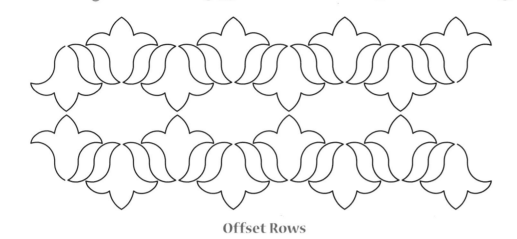

Offset Rows

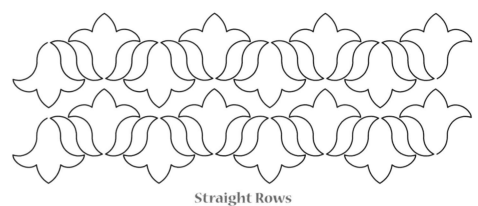

Straight Rows

5"

Nesting Rows

Straight Rows

5"

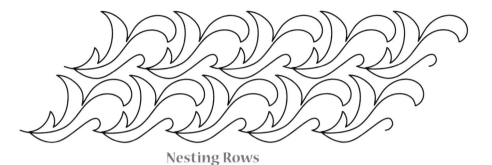

Nesting Rows

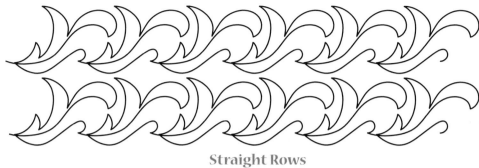

Straight Rows

3½" E F M T

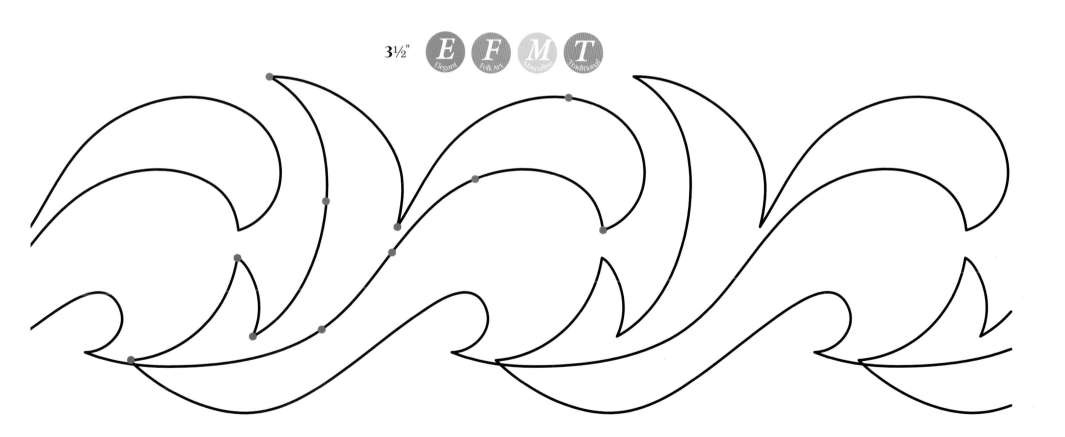

Offset Rows

Straight Rows

4"

5"

E
Elegant

F
Folk Art

M
Masculine

Mirrored and Offset Rows   **Straight Rows**

3½" E F T

Secondary Design

3"

3"

3½"

3"

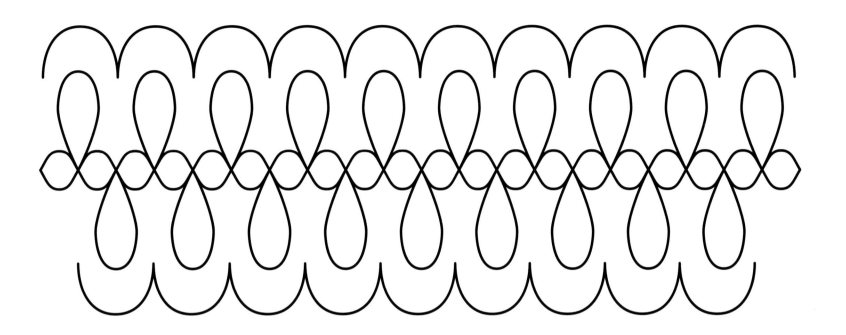

3½"

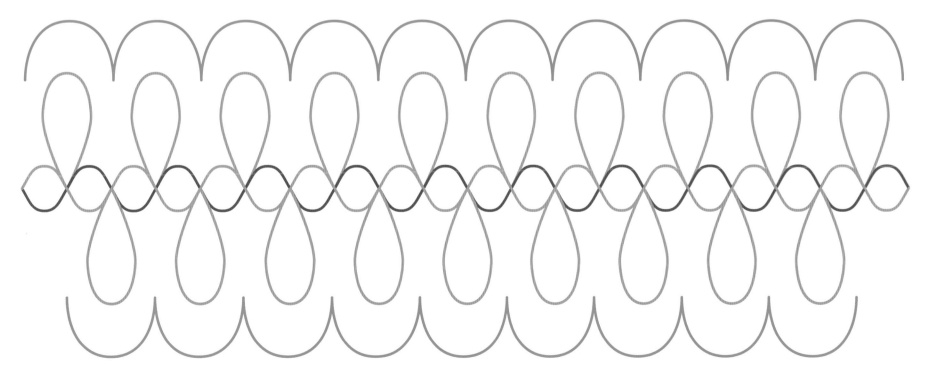

Stitching Sequence

7"

Line 1

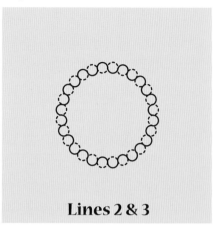

Lines 2 & 3

Line 4

Line 5

Stitching Sequence

Line 1

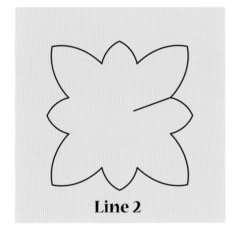

Line 2

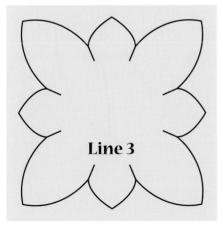

Line 3

7"

3"

4"

4½"

G *Geometric* J *Juvenile* M *Masculine*

Stitching Sequence

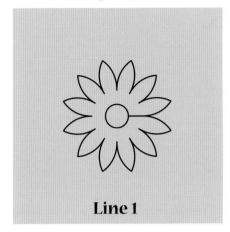

Line 1

Line 2

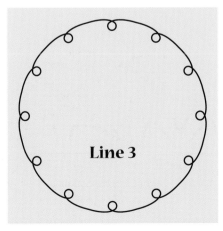

Line 3

7"

2½"

G Geometric   **F** Folk Art

2½"

G Geometric   **F** Folk Art

2½"

E Elegant   **M** Masculine

4½"

E Elegant

G Geometric

F Folk Art

M Masculine

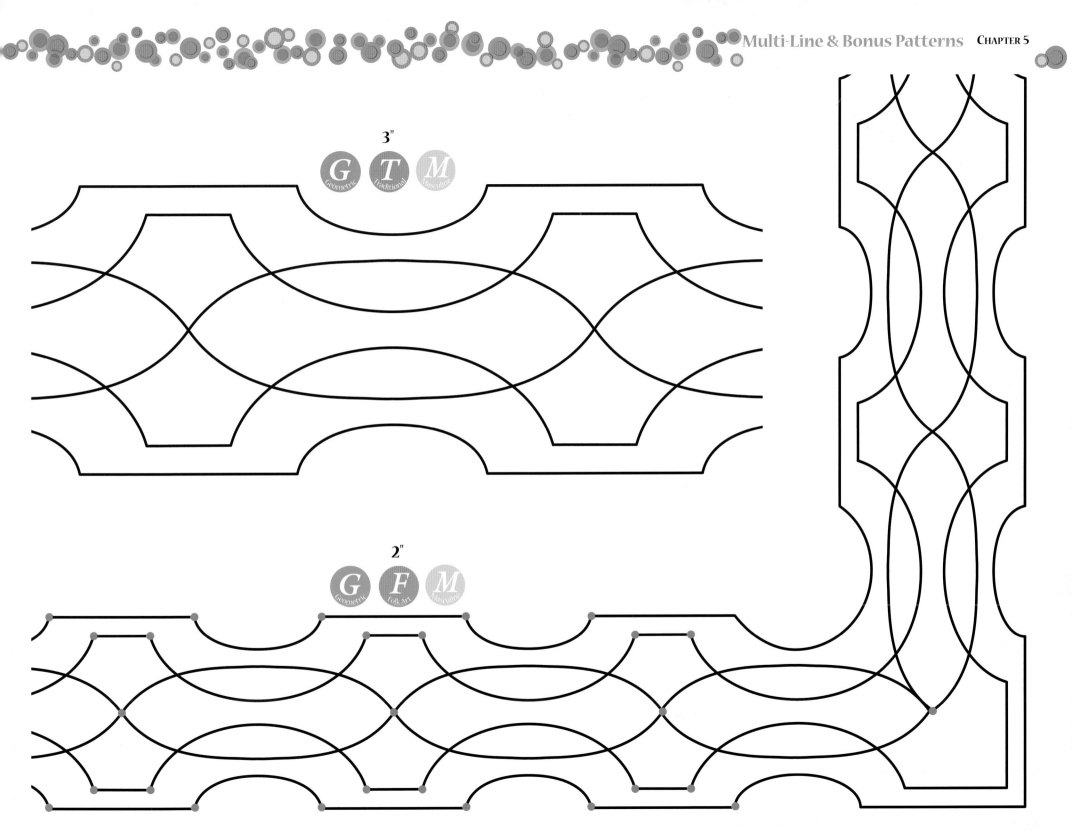

3"

2"

E Elegant G Geometric F Folk Art T Traditional

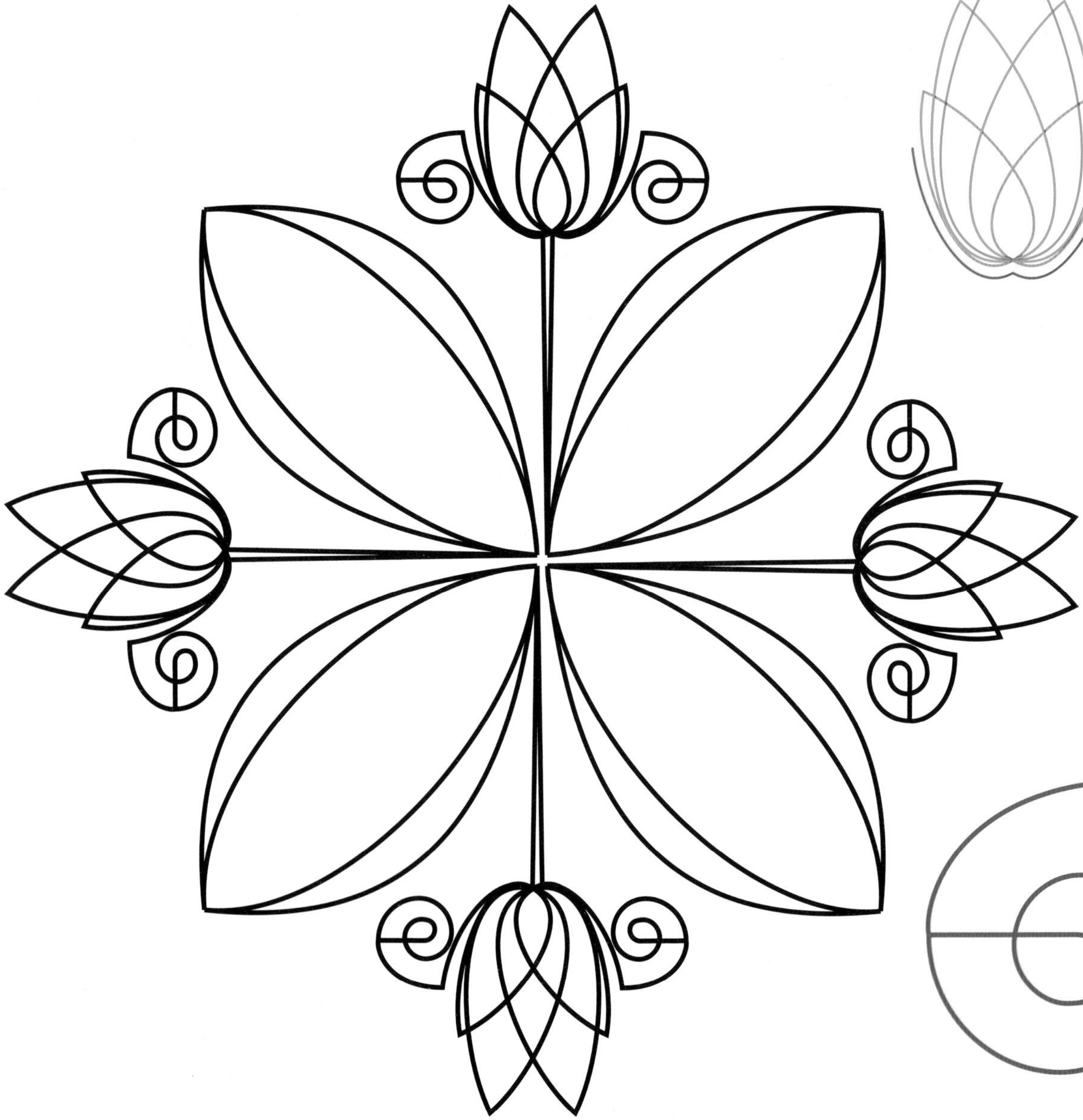

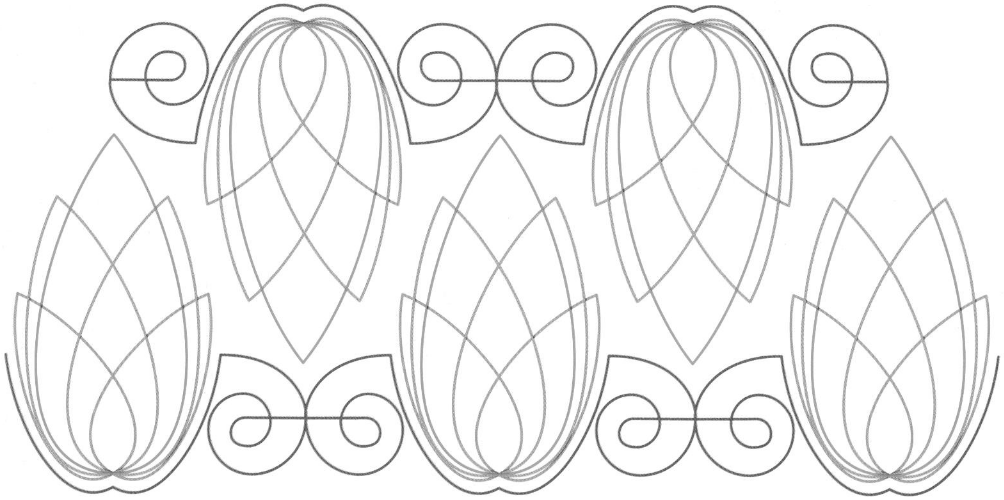

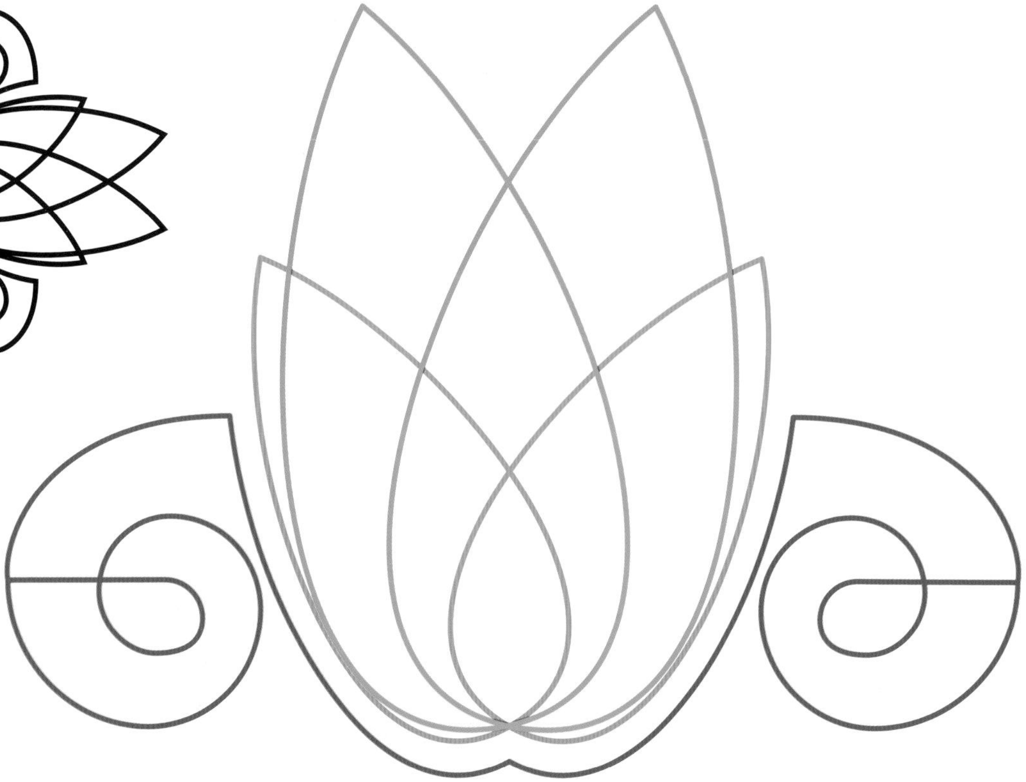

Spotlight on Quilting

Class Ideas & Special Events

The focus and popularity of machine quilting is at an all time high. Quilters everywhere need classes and support from teachers and their local shops. Focusing the spotlight on quilting for your students is as easy as expanding the classes and events you have already planned and organized.

One hour addition

Add one hour to each piecing technique class to present ideas for quilting and completing the project. Be sure to quilt the class sample and present suggestions on other variations for quilting each project. Include quilting designs, batting, and thread choices.

One class addition (2-3 hours)

Add one class to the end of a multi-part class to present ideas for quilting and completing the project. Allocating a whole 2-3 hour class allows enough time to guide students through the three Building Blocks for successful machine quilting.

How should I quilt this quilt?

Half day class - no machines

Each student should bring a completed quilt top to class. Use unquilted shop samples to demonstrate the Building Blocks of successful quilting. Demo the techniques for resizing and creating paper stencils with Golden Threads Quilting Paper. Guide your students through analyzing, selecting, and auditioning quilting patterns for their individual tops.

Stepping Stones to Free-Motion Quilting

Half day class with machines

Every student should start with the first Stepping Stone and progress to the last Stepping Stone, quilting on a mini-quilt practice sandwich. Mark the quilting patterns with dots to help identify familiar shapes. Allow the students to progress at their own pace. Everyone will leave class with increased quilting confidence, ability, and the tools needed to continue to improve after the class has ended.

Quilting Gallery

Reserve a display space in your shop or classroom and showcase quilts from a popular class that highlight machine quilting. Students who have quilted their projects will be honored when asked to be a part of this gallery. Hang several uniquely quilted examples to illustrate how varying patterns and thread choices can enhance the same pieced quilt top. This is a perfect way to individualize Block of the Month promotions and fabric kits.

Quilting Challenge

To advertise an upcoming class, hang the unquilted class sample and provide a suggestion board/box and encourage your customers to help plan the quilting. Ask them to suggest areas for the quilting, quilting designs, thread color choices, etc. During the actual class discuss some of the suggestions, have the class pick their favorites, and promise to quilt it and hang the quilted project in your Quilting Gallery. Encourage your students to quilt their projects and schedule a "Quilter's Show & Tell."

Quilting Club

Revive the quilting "Bee" and encourage your customers to come together, enjoy each other's company, and get some quilting done. Quilting clubs can be formed for hand, machine, and frame quilters. Make it easy—advertise a consistent day of the week/month and time to encourage an informal gathering for quilters to socialize and learn from each other and quilt. Just get the word out, have a knowledgeable quilter available to answer questions, and have a good selection of notions, quilting supplies, and designs. Keep it relaxed and fun for everyone!

Golden Threads Quilting Paper, Quilter's Assistance Proportion Scale,
The Ultimate Pounce®, Pantograph patterns, pattern packs, stencils, books, and other supplies
available at local quilt, fabric, and craft shops, quilting frame and sewing machine dealers, catalogs, or order direct.

About The Author

After quilting for several years, Cheryl felt limited by the lack of new patterns available to longarm quilters. The pursuit of building a library of quilting designs took Cheryl's company from quilting to publishing quilting designs. She became acquainted with the quilting designs by Keryn Emmerson of Australia, who was searching for a publisher that would service the longarm industry. Golden Threads continues to publish originally designed quilting patterns from prominent United States and Australian artists.

Cheryl and her husband, Jim, also own Powell Publications. They purchased the company in 2002, which expanded their listing of designers and patterns. The broad range of products all focused on quilting patterns makes their business unique. Stencils, pantographs, pattern packs, books, quilted garments, and notions enable them to service all quilters—from hand or sewing machine quilters to those with home quilting systems or longarm machines. With a broad range of talented designers, each with their own style, they are sure to have something that appeals to every quilter.

Cheryl also works with Husqvarna Viking and Pfaff Sewing Machines as a consultant who helps customers with their home quilting systems. In this capacity, she travels nationwide to work with educators and dealers, and to present consumer seminars. This role has given her the insight needed to develop new products, including this book, that are tailored to meet the needs of the home quilter. Her involvement in this industry has also opened Cheryl's eyes to the needs of embroiderers and seamstresses. She plans to continue developing new products that will meet the needs of quilters, embroiderers, and seamstresses alike.

Residing in Illinois, Cheryl and Jim work full time in the business. Their three sons have all participated in the family business, rolling pantographs, filling orders, taking inventory, and occasionally attending quilt shows. The company continues to expand through a new pattern and technique book series published in cooperation with the American Quilter's Society.

Other Books

This is only a small selection of the books available from the American Quilter's Society. AQS books are known worldwide for timely topics, clear writing, beautiful color photos, and for accurate illustrations and patterns. The following books are available from your local bookseller or quilt shop.

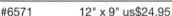

#6571   12" x 9" us$24.95

#6896   us$22.95

#6678   12" x 9" us$22.95

#6907   us$21.95

#6800   us$22.95

#6806   us$21.95

#6803   12" x 9" us$22.95

#6006   us$25.95

#6509   12" x 9" us$22.95

Look for these books nationally.
Call or **Visit** our Web site at

1-800-626-5420
www.AmericanQuilter.com

Products

Companion Pattern Packs from the Authors Who Wrote the Books!

Ready-to-use individual 11" x 17" sheets of selected patterns in a variety of real sizes.

#32013   us$16.95

PLUS Bonus Materials

#32012   us$16.95

- Designs • How-to Advice
- Popular Motifs

Golden Threads Quilting Paper
Trace and Sew Tear-Away Stencils

#32001   12" x 20 yds. $7.50
#32002   18" x 20 yds. $10.95
#32003   24" x 20 yds. $12.95

Available at quilt shops, fabric stores, quilting frame and sewing machine dealers, catalogs, or order direct.

Quilter's Assistant Proportional Scale
#35023 . . . . $5.95

GOLDEN THREADS
www.goldenthreads.com